THINKING OF YOU

THINKING OF YOU

*L*oyalty is the most important thing you can give someone. Truth, trust, friendship and very often love all depend on it.

ELVIS PRESLEY

*Y*ou can make more friends in two months by becoming interested in other people than you can in two years by trying to get people interested in you.

DALE CARNEGIE

*W*herever you go, whatever you do—always make friends with the cook.

JOHN RATZENBERGER

*G*ive what you have. To someone, it may be better than you dare think.

HENRY WADSWORTH LONGFELLOW

*T*he grand essentials to happiness in this life are something to do, someone to love, and something to hope for.

JOSEPH ADDISON

*G*ood coffee is like friendship: rich and warm and strong.

PAN-AMERICAN COFFEE BUREAU

*W*e can only learn to love by loving.

IRIS MURDOCK

*I*t's that wonderful, old-fashioned idea that others come first and you come second. This was the whole ethic by which I was brought up. Others matter more than you do, *so don't fuss, dear; get on with it.*

AUDREY HEPBURN

The love we give away is the only love we keep.

ELBERT HUBBARD

Friendship is constant in all other things
Save in the office and affairs of love.

SHAKESPEARE,
Much Ado About Nothing

You can always tell a real friend: when you've made a fool of yourself he doesn't feel you've done a permanent job.

LAURENCE J. PETER

Love your enemy—it'll drive him nuts.

ANONYMOUS

*L*aughter is the best remedy for the sick at heart.

EVELYN BEILENSON

*L*ife in common among people who love each other is the ideal of happiness.

GEORGE SAND

*I*t's a funny thing about life: If you refuse to accept anything but the best, you often get it.

W. SOMERSET MAUGHAM

[*T*here's] a line from a play: *To love somebody is to know that you can tell everything and not be laughed at, and not be judged.* I think that really says a lot.

HUME CRONYN

*T*he essence of true friendship is to make allowance for another's little lapses.

DAVID STOREY

*Y*ou can't always expect a certain result, but you can expect to do your best.

ANITA HILL

*D*on't let anyone tell you what you *can't* do. If you don't succeed, let it be because of you. Don't blame it on other people.

EARVIN "MAGIC" JOHNSON

*I*f you have made mistakes, even serious ones, there is always another chance for you. What we call failure is not the falling down, but the staying down.

MARY PICKFORD

*W*hat is life but a series of inspired follies? The difficulty is to find them to do. Never lose a chance: it doesn't come every day.

GEORGE BERNARD SHAW

*D*on't give in.
Fight for your future.
Independence is the only solution.
Women are as good as men.
Onward!
You don't have too much money but you do have *independent spirits.*
Knowledge! Education! Don't give in!
Make your own trail.
Don't moan.
Don't complain.
Think positively.

KATHARINE HEPBURN,
describing her mother's philosophy of life

*T*o feel valued and nurtured can change the course of a life.

DR. MICHAEL A. CARRERA

*P*leasure is very seldom found where it is sought; our brightest blazes of gladness are commonly kindled by unexpected sparks.

SAMUEL JOHNSON

*W*e must never be bitter—if we indulge in hate, the new order will only be the old order. . . . We must meet hate with love, physical force with soul force.

MARTIN LUTHER KING, JR.

*E*very man feels instinctively that all the beautiful sentiments in the world weigh less than a single lovely action.

JAMES RUSSELL LOWELL

*I*t's nice to be important, but it's more important to be nice.

TRINI LOPEZ

*T*he world is more beautiful when you hold hands and walk together.

EVELYN LOEB

*H*old a true friend with both your hands.

NIGERIAN PROVERB

*D*on't try so much to form your character—it's like trying to pull open a tight, tender young rose. Live as you like best, and your character will take care of itself.

HENRY JAMES,
Portrait of a Lady

I don't know the key to success, but the key to failure is to try to please everyone.

BILL COSBY

$\mathcal{T}$here is always hope for an individual who stops to do some serious thinking about life.

KATHERINE LOGAN

$\mathcal{J}$ust as a sunbeam can't separate itself from the sun, and a wave can't separate itself from the ocean, we can't separate ourselves from one another. We are all part of a vast sea of love, one indivisible divine mind.

MARIANNE WILLIAMSON

$\mathcal{T}$reat the person as if they were your child.

JOHN BESS

$\mathcal{N}$ever get involved with someone who wants to change you.

QUENTIN CRISP

*I*f you think you can, you can. And if you think you can't, you're right.

MARY KAY ASH

*A*nd the trouble is, if you don't risk anything, you risk even more.

ERICA JONG

*W*hen we start at the center of ourselves, we discover something worthwhile extending toward the periphery of the circle.

ANNE MORROW LINDBERGH

*A*s long as you believe in yourself, others will.

CYNDA WILLIAMS

*T*ry to take each day and each task as they come, breaking them down into manageable pieces for action while struggling to see the whole. And don't think you have to "win" immediately or even at all to make a difference.

MARIAN WRIGHT EDELMAN

*T*o love what you do and feel that it matters—how could anything be more fun?

KATHERINE GRAHAM

*H*appiness sneaks in through a door you didn't know you left open.

JOHN BARRYMORE

*A*n inexhaustible good nature is one of the most precious gifts of heaven, spreading itself like oil over the troubled sea of thought, and keeping the mind smooth and equable in the roughest weather.

WASHINGTON IRVING

A man's character is judged by that of the friends whose society he takes pleasure in.

AESOP

*Y*ou do not have to be rich to be generous. If he has the spirit of true generosity, a pauper can give like a prince.

CORINNE U. WELLS

*G*ood friends are good for your health.

IRWIN SARASON

*W*hy be influenced by a person when you already are one?

MARTIN MULL

*D*o not aim lower than your potential. Few people have ever attained a higher level than the one to which they aspired.

PATRICIA HARRIS

*L*ife is too short to be little.

BENJAMIN DISRAELI

*T*he wise man will make more opportunities than he finds.

FRANCIS BACON

*Y*ou've got to love what's lovable and hate what's hateable. It takes brains to see the difference.

ROBERT FROST

I think that, for all of us, as we grow older we must discipline ourselves to continue expanding, broadening, learning, keeping our minds active and open. And that's the challenge each of us has earned.

CLINT EASTWOOD

*D*on't despair, not even over the fact that you don't despair.

KAFKA

A friend who cannot at a pinch remember a thing or two that never happened is as bad as one who does not know how to forget.

SAMUEL BUTLER

*T*rue friends, like ivy and the wall Both stand together, and together fall.

FRANCIS BACON

$\mathscr{O}$ne loyal friend is worth ten thousand relatives.

EURIPIDES

$\mathscr{T}$he first duty of love is to listen.

PAUL TILLICH

$\mathscr{T}$he real marriage of true minds is for any two people to possess a sense of humor or irony pitched in exactly the same key, so that their joint glances at any subject cross like interarching search lights.

EDITH WHARTON

$\mathscr{N}$o man who has once heartily and wholly laughed can be altogether irreclaimably bad.

THOMAS CARLYLE

$\mathcal{H}$ard work and self discipline will get you everywhere.

HELEN GURLEY BROWN

$\mathcal{I}$ think if you have a talent, then you must absolutely give it to people as long as you can.

INGRID BERGMAN

$\mathcal{I}$ think that being relaxed at all times, and I mean relaxed, not collapsed, can add to the happiness and duration of one's life and looks. And relaxed people are fun to be around.

CARY GRANT

$\mathcal{E}$ njoy life—this is not a dress rehearsal.

BUMPER STICKER

$\mathcal{E}$very day's a kick!

OPRAH WINFREY

$\mathcal{T}$here is only one happiness in life, to love and be loved.

GEORGE SAND

$\mathcal{T}$he man who treasures his friends is usually solid gold himself.

MARJORIE HOLMES

$\mathcal{Y}$ou can choose your friends, but you only have one mother.

MAX SHULMAN

$\mathcal{F}$riendship requires great communication between friends. Otherwise, it can neither be born nor exist.

SAINT FRANCIS DE SALES

$\mathcal{W}$hen one's own problems are unsolvable and all best efforts frustrated, it is lifesaving to listen to other people's problems.

SUZANNE MASSIE

$\mathcal{T}$o my friend: May you live as long as you like, and have all that you like as long as you live.

ANONYMOUS

$\mathcal{N}$o man is useless while he has a friend.

ROBERT LOUIS STEVENSON

$\mathcal{O}$f course platonic friendship is possible—
but only between husband and wife.

ANONYMOUS

$\mathcal{D}$on't compromise yourself. You are all
you've got.

JANIS JOPLIN

$\mathcal{O}$ne of the greatest diseases is to be
nobody to anybody.

MOTHER TERESA

$\mathcal{F}$riendship multiplies the good of life and
divides the evil. 'Tis the sole remedy against
misfortune, the very ventilation of the soul.

BALTASAR GRACIÁN

$\mathscr{H}$ave a blast while you last.

HOLLIS STACY

$\mathscr{I}$ love everything that's old: old friends, old times, old manners, old books, old wine.

OLIVER GOLDSMITH,
She Stoops to Conquer

$\mathscr{T}$here are two worlds; the world that we can measure with line and rule, and the world that we feel with our hearts and imagination.

LEIGH HUNT

$\mathscr{H}$appiness is experienced when your life gives you what you are willing to accept.

KEN KEYES

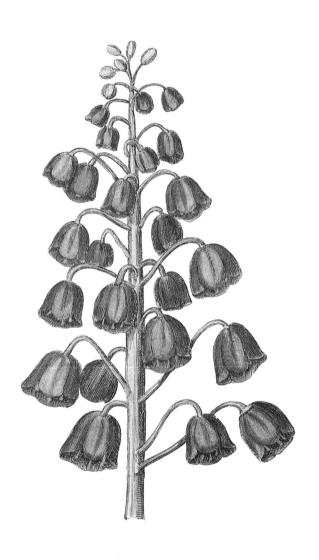

*N*othing in life is to be feared. It is only to be understood.

MARIE CURIE

*L*ife was meant to be lived, and curiosity must be kept alive. One must never, for whatever reason, turn his back on life.

ELEANOR ROOSEVELT

*T*here are risks and costs to a program of action. But they are far less than the long-range risks and costs of comfortable inaction.

JOHN F. KENNEDY

*G*reater love hath no man than this, that a man lay down his life for his friends.

JOHN 15:13 (KJV)

$\mathcal{I}$t is common sense to take a method and try it. If it fails, admit it frankly and try another. But above all, try something.

FRANKLIN D. ROOSEVELT

$\mathcal{G}$ive plenty of what is given to you,
And listen to pity's call;
Don't think the little you give is great
And the much you get is small.

PHOEBE CARY

$\mathcal{T}$o improve is to change; to be perfect is to change often.

WINSTON CHURCHILL

$\mathcal{E}$ach friend represents a world in us, a world possibly not born until they arrive, and it is only by this meeting that a new world is born.

ANAÏS NIN

$\mathcal{O}$nce the mind releases itself into love, there are suddenly a thousand obvious ways to show it.

HUGH AND GAYLE PRATHER

$\mathcal{T}$hree-fourths of the people you will ever meet are hungering and thirsting for sympathy. Give it to them, and they will love you.

DALE CARNEGIE

$\mathcal{N}$o one is useless in this world who lightens the burdens of another.

CHARLES DICKENS

$\mathcal{A}$ man should never be ashamed to own he has been in the wrong, which is but saying in other words that he is wiser today than he was yesterday.

JONATHAN SWIFT

*T*reat your friends as you do your picture, and place them in their best light.

JENNIE JEROME CHURCHILL

*I*f a friendship is vital, it's subject to change. In fact, it's vital only if it *does* change. A woman I once knew said a wise thing: *Never fight with anybody you don't love.*

JACK NICHOLSON

*Y*our truest friends are those who visit you in prison or in hospital.

MOROCCAN PROVERB

A friendship is ultimately a more interesting exploration than a love affair, because it lacks the spur of sex and, one presumes, is forged in a cooler furnace.

JOE FLAHERTY

$\mathcal{W}$e must not waste life in devising means. It is better to plan less and do more.

WILLIAM ELLERY CHANNING

$\mathcal{T}$he capacity for friendship usually goes with highly developed civilization.

MARGARET MEAD

$\mathcal{E}$veryone's got to be different. You can't copy anybody and end up with anything. If you copy, it means you're working without any real feeling. And without feeling, whatever you do amounts to nothing.

BILLIE HOLIDAY

$\mathcal{P}$erhaps loving something is the only starting place there is for making your life your own.

ALICE KOLLER

$\mathcal{O}$ur main goals are to find an authentic sharing kind of humanity. Love, loyalty, generosity, friendship: These are the things that are at the core of civilized life. But we are deflected constantly by the sheer multitude of duties, solicitation and multitude of options.

ROBERT PAUL MOHAN

$\mathcal{T}$he future comes one day at a time.

DEAN ACHESON

$\mathcal{H}$e who has a thousand friends has not a
   friend to spare,
And he who has one enemy will meet
   him everywhere.

RALPH WALDO EMERSON

$\mathcal{S}$tyle is style is style is you.

GERTRUDE STEIN

$\mathcal{F}$ind the grain of truth in criticism—chew it and swallow it.

D. SUTTEN

$\mathcal{M}$y idea of good company, Mr. Elliot, is a company of clever, well-informed people, who have a great deal of conversation; that is what I call good company. You are mistaken, said he, gently, *that is not good company; that is the best.*

JANE AUSTEN,
Persuasion

$\mathcal{T}$o be rich in friends is to be poor in nothing.

LILIAN WHITING

$\mathcal{Y}$ou are a child of the universe no less than the trees and the stars; you have a right to be here.

ANONYMOUS

*I*n the main, sociability is a knack; but it is also partly a skill, to be learned and cultivated like any other. Therefore, friendship returned is almost invariably equal to friendship given.

JOSEPH W. ALSOP

*Y*ou must act in your friend's interest whether it pleases him or not; the object of love is to serve, not to win.

WOODROW WILSON

*N*o one's head aches when he is comforting another.

INDIAN PROVERB

*O*nly what you have not given can be lacking in any situation.

MARIANNE WILLIAMSON

*F*riends are people you can talk to . . . without words, when you have to.

ELVIS PRESLEY

*W*hen men are friendly even water is sweet.

CHINESE PROVERB

*S*ooner or later you've heard what all your best friends have to say. Then comes the tolerance of real love.

NED ROREM

*O*h, love is real enough, you will find it some day, but it has one arch-enemy, and that is life.

JEAN ANOUILH

$\mathscr{Y}$ou cannot be friends upon any other terms than upon the terms of equality.

WOODROW WILSON

$\mathscr{W}$e talked about quality things like honesty, integrity, love and respect. I tried to live that example for them, and when you do, it catches on.

VIRGINIA KELLEY,
mother of Bill Clinton, on raising her sons

$\mathscr{T}$he best friend is likely to acquire the best wife, because a good marriage is based on the talent of friendship.

NIETZSCHE

$\mathscr{L}$ove conquers all things except poverty and a toothache.

MAE WEST

*T*he motto should not be: *forgive one another;* rather *understand one another.*

EMMA GOLDMAN

*Y*ou have to learn to take political attacks seriously but not personally, so that you don't let them interfere with what you are.

HILLARY CLINTON

*R*ead. Not just what you have to read for class or work, but to learn from the wisdom and joys and mistakes of others. No time is ever wasted if you have a book along as a companion.

MARIAN WRIGHT EDELMAN

*S*he'll bring you the aspirin, the OJ, the chicken soup. She very much knows what's going on in her friends' lives—which is why they adore her.

CONNIE FRIEBERG,
speaking of her friend, Teri Garr

*T*reat others as ends, never as means.

DAG HAMMARSKJÖLD

*W*e cannot tell the precise moment when friendship is formed. As in filling a vessel drop by drop, there is at last a drop which makes it run over; so in a series of kindnesses there is at last one which makes the heart run over.

SAMUEL JOHNSON

*W*hen you really want love you will find it waiting for you.

OSCAR WILDE

*S*ir, more than kisses, letters mingle
  souls;
For, thus friends absent speak.

JOHN DONNE

*O*f all the things which wisdom provides to make life entirely happy, much the greatest is the possession of friendship.

EPICURUS

I can better trust those who helped to relieve the gloom of my dark hours than those who are so ready to enjoy with me the sunshine of my prosperity.

ULYSSES S. GRANT

*P*ersons are to be loved; things are to be used.

REUEL HOWE

*W*hen two people love each other, they don't look at each other, they look in the same direction.

GINGER ROGERS

*F*riendship is to have the latchkey of another's mind.

EDGAR J. GOODSPEED

*T*he feeling of friendship is like that of being comfortably filled with roast beef; love, like being enlivened with champagne.

SAMUEL JOHNSON

*M*any things cause pain which would cause pleasure if you regarded their advantages.

BALTASAR GRACIÁN

*G*enuine friends are proved by adversity.

AESOP

$\mathcal{I}$'m a big believer that you have to nourish any relationship. I am still very much a part of my friends' lives and they are very much a part of my life.

NANCY REAGAN

$\mathcal{F}$riends can never be family, but some of the things you go through can make you even closer.

ELVIS PRESLEY

$\mathcal{A}$bsence makes the heart grow fonder.

SEXTUS PROPERTIUS

$\mathcal{F}$riends, and I mean real friends—
   reserve nothing;
The property of one belongs to the other.

EURIPIDES

*I*t may be more important to have at least
one person with whom we can share open and
honest thoughts and feelings than it is to have a
whole network of more superficial relationships.

DR. BLAIR JUSTICE

*M*emory, my dear Cecily, is the diary we all
carry about with us.

OSCAR WILDE

*S*he is such a good friend that she would
throw all her acquaintances into the water for
the pleasure of fishing them out.

TALLEYRAND,
of Mme. de Staël

*A*nimals are such agreeable friends—they
ask no questions, they pass no criticisms.

GEORGE ELIOT

A friend must not be injured, even in jest.

PUBLILIUS SYRUS

*W*hoever gives a small coin to a poor man has six blessings bestowed upon him, but he who speaks a kind word to him obtains eleven blessings.

TALMUD

*A*nybody can sympathize with the sufferings of a friend, but it requires a very fine nature to sympathize with a friend's success.

OSCAR WILDE

A satisfying life has a harmony. Not a harmony in the sense of ease or a lack of turmoil; a harmony in the sense of being right for your time.

JOHN MUNSCHAUER

$\mathcal{T}$alk not of love, it gives me pain,
For love has been my foe;
He bound me with an iron chain,
And plunged me deep in woe.
But friendship's pure and lasting joys,
My heart was formed to prove.

AGNES CRAIG

$\mathcal{A}$ friend is one who does not laugh when
you are in a ridiculous position.

SIR ARTHUR HELPS

$\mathcal{S}$he's the kind of woman who'd go through
hell, high water, or a paper shredder for a pal.

KATHI MAIO,
Feminist in the Dark

$\mathcal{N}$othing is as dangerous as an ignorant
friend; a wise enemy is to be preferred.

JEAN DE LA FONTAINE

$\mathcal{F}$riendship needs no words—it is a loneliness relieved of the anguish of loneliness.

DAG HAMMARSKJÖLD

$\mathcal{I}$ cannot forgive my friends for dying; I do not find these vanishing acts of theirs at all amusing.

LOGAN PEARSALL SMITH

$\mathcal{C}$ertainly, my dear, friendship is a mighty pretty invention, and, next to love, gives of all things the greatest spirit to society.

FRANCES BROOKE

$\mathcal{M}$ighty proud I am that I am able to have a spare bed for my friends.

SAMUEL PEPYS

$\mathcal{T}$hough you are in your shining days,
Voices among the crowd
And new friends busy with your praise,
Be not unkind or proud,
But think about old friends the most:
Time's bitter flood will rise,
Your beauty perish and be lost
For all eyes but these eyes.

WILLIAM BUTLER YEATS,
*The Lover Pleads with
His Friend for Old Friends*

$\mathcal{T}$he very best thing is good talk, and the
thing that helps it most is friendship.

HENRY VAN DYKE

$\mathcal{W}$hen you're with someone who's supportive
and adores you, it can't help but make you
feel—and look—younger.

CHERYL TIEGS

$\mathscr{L}$ove is what makes a crowd disappear when you're with someone.

ELVIS PRESLEY

$\mathscr{I}$f you can't say anything good about someone, sit right here by me.

ALICE ROOSEVELT LONGWORTH,
embroidered on a pillow

$\mathscr{B}$e still when you have nothing to say; when genuine passion moves you, say what you've got to say, and say it hot.

D. H. LAWRENCE

$\mathscr{S}$piritual energy brings compassion into the real world. With compassion, we see benevolently our own human condition and the condition of our fellow human beings. We drop prejudice. We withhold judgment.

CHRISTINA BALDWIN

$\mathcal{G}$etting people to like you is merely the other side of liking them.

NORMAN VINCENT PEALE

$\mathcal{W}$ithout friendship and the openness and trust that go with it, skills are barren and knowledge may become an unguided missile.

FRANK H. T. RHODES

$\mathcal{A}$cceptance does not preclude change, it precludes remaining in conflict.

HUGH AND GAYLE PRATHER

$\mathcal{T}$he telephone is a great knee-jerk machine, but if you really want to tell someone how you feel, you need the slowness of a letter. In a society where everything is fast, it's like going out in the country and looking up at the stars.

NICK BANTOCK

*I*f we let our friend become cold and selfish and exacting without a remonstrance, we are no true lover, no true friend.

HARRIET BEECHER STOWE

*T*here is no end. There is no beginning. There is only the infinite passion of life.

FEDERICO FELLINI

*I*t is not easy to find happiness in ourselves, and it is not possible to find it elsewhere.

AGNES REPPLIER

*I*n fact, you cannot *lead* the Simple Life; it must take you by the hand.

JANET ASHBEE

*T*here is no stronger bond of friendship than a mutual enemy.

J. P. MORGAN

*F*ame is the scentless sunflower,
  with gaudy crown of gold;
But friendship is the breathing rose,
  with sweets in every fold.

OLIVER WENDELL HOLMES

*T*hy friend has a friend, and thy friend's friend has a friend; be discreet.

TALMUD

*T*he joy is in the journey and not arriving at the destination.

DIANE SAWYER

$\mathcal{T}$he trick is to make sure you don't die waiting for prosperity to come.

LEE IACOCCA

$\mathcal{I}$t really boils down to this: that all life is interrelated. We are all caught in an inescapable network of mutuality, tied into a single garment of destiny. Whatever affects one directly, affects all indirectly.

MARTIN LUTHER KING, JR.

$\mathcal{D}$on't be afraid of missing opportunities. Behind every failure is an opportunity somebody wishes *they* had missed.

LILY TOMLIN

$\mathcal{I}$f you have to ask how much friendship costs, you probably cannot afford it.

CHRISTOPHER LEHMANN-HAUPT

$\mathcal{L}$ife without a friend; death without a witness.

GEORGE HERBERT

$\mathcal{A}$ friend can tell you things you don't want to tell yourself.

FRANCIS WARD WELLER,
Boat Song

$\mathcal{W}$ithout wearing any mask we are conscious of, we have a special face for each friend.

OLIVER WENDELL HOLMES

$\mathcal{T}$he loneliest woman in the world is a woman without a close woman friend.

TONI MORRISON

$\mathcal{B}$lessed are they who have the gift of making friends for it is one of God's best gifts. It involves many things, but above all, the power of going out of one's self, and appreciating whatever is noble and loving in another.

THOMAS HUGHES

$\mathcal{I}$ basically believe that every person has an intrinsic value and that you have to try to find out what yours is.

BILL CLINTON

$\mathcal{O}$ld friends are best. King James used to call for his old shoes; they were easiest for his feet.

JOHN SELDEN

$\mathcal{A}$ friend in power is a friend lost.

HENRY ADAMS

*F*oolish people like to test the bonds of their friendships, pulling upon them to see how much strain they will stand. When they snap, it is as if friendship itself had been proved unworthy. But the truth is that good friendships are fragile and precious things.

RANDOLPH S. BOURNE

*T*wo chambers has the heart,
Wherein dwell Joy and Sorrow;
When Joy awakes in one,
Then slumbers Sorrow in the other.
O Joy, take care!
Speak softly,
Lest you awaken Sorrow.

HERMAN NEUMAN

*I*t's never too late—never too late to start over, never too late to be happy.

JANE FONDA

*L*ike my father said in his simple catechism, trust your future to the things you love.

DIANE SAWYER

$\mathcal{I}$t is the friends that you can call at 4 A.M. that matter.

MARLENE DIETRICH

$\mathcal{G}$entle ladies, you will remember till old age what we did together in our brilliant youth!

SAPPHO

$\mathcal{W}$ell, this is the end of a perfect day,
Near the end of a journey, too;
But it leaves a thought that is big and
    strong,
With a wish that is kind and true.
For mem'ry has painted this perfect day
With colors that never fade,
And we find, at the end of a perfect day,
The soul of a friend we've made.

CARRIE JACOBS BOND

*F*riendship is the shadow of the evening,
which strengthens with the setting sun of life.

JEAN DE LA FONTAINE

*T*ry to live in the present; don't carry around
unnecessary burdens from a yesterday you will
not live again or a tomorrow that is not
guaranteed.

MARIAN WRIGHT EDELMAN

I am not of that feather to shake off
My friend when he must need me.

SHAKESPEARE,
Timon of Athens

*U*s can spend the day celebrating each
other.

ALICE WALKER,
The Color Purple

*D*on't give up! Surround yourself with people who are energetic and disciplined. Surround yourselves with ambitious, positive people.

EARVIN "MAGIC" JOHNSON

I'm an idealist. I don't know where I am headed but I'm on my way!

CARL SANDBURG

*B*ut I don't know, I still believe good endings are possible, something to strive for, something to be proud of.

DIANE KEATON